Guess Who's...
Scary!

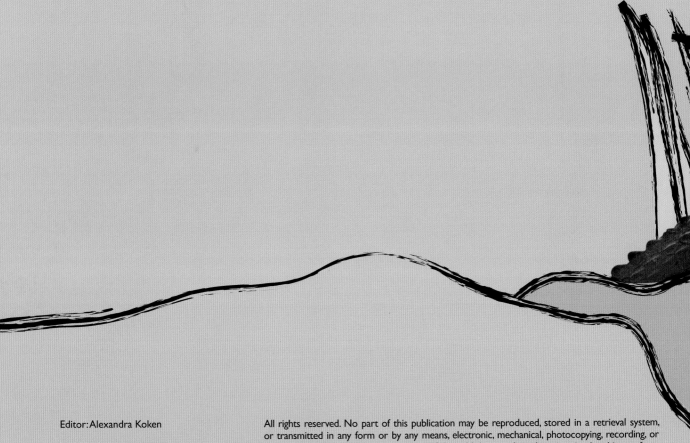

Picture credits
(t=top, b=bottom, l=left, r=right, c=centre, fc=front cover)
FLPA: 3 Bernd Rohrschneider, 4–5 Paul Sawyer, 14–15 Neil Bowman
Nature PL: 6–7, 16l Tony Heald, 8–9 16b Brandon Cole, 12–13 John Cancalosi
NHPA: 10–11, 17tl, 18l Adrian Hepworth
Shutterstock: 18tr Arnoud Quanjer, 18b, 20 M.R., 19 Michael Woodruff

Editor: Alexandra Koken

Copyright © QED Publishing 2012

First published in the UK in 2012 by
QED Publishing
A Quarto Group company
230 City Road
London EC1V 2TT

www.qed-publishing.co.uk

A catalogue record for this book is available from the British Library.

ISBN 978 1 84835 842 3

Printed in China

Guess Who's...
Scary!

Camilla de la Bédoyère and Fiona Hajée

QED

QED Publishing

Who has big paws
with sharp claws?

Who loves
honey?

a bald
face?

When I stand up I am huge!
I live in the forest and
like to be left alone.

I do!
I am a brown bear.

Who likes to feed on dead animals?

Who is a big fish with sharp teeth?

Who has eight
small eyes?

Who has eight
hairy legs?

Who can make a rattling
sound with its tail?

Who can smell
with its tongue?

Who can slither
and hiss?

Who is waiting for lunch to walk by?

Who is big, strong and fast?

I am!

I am a crocodile.

Look through the book
to find the scary animal
that matches each clue.

I am a spider with
[eig]ht legs and eight
[...] ame begins
[with let]ter t.

My jaws snap shut.
I can't chew my food so
I swallow it in big gulps!

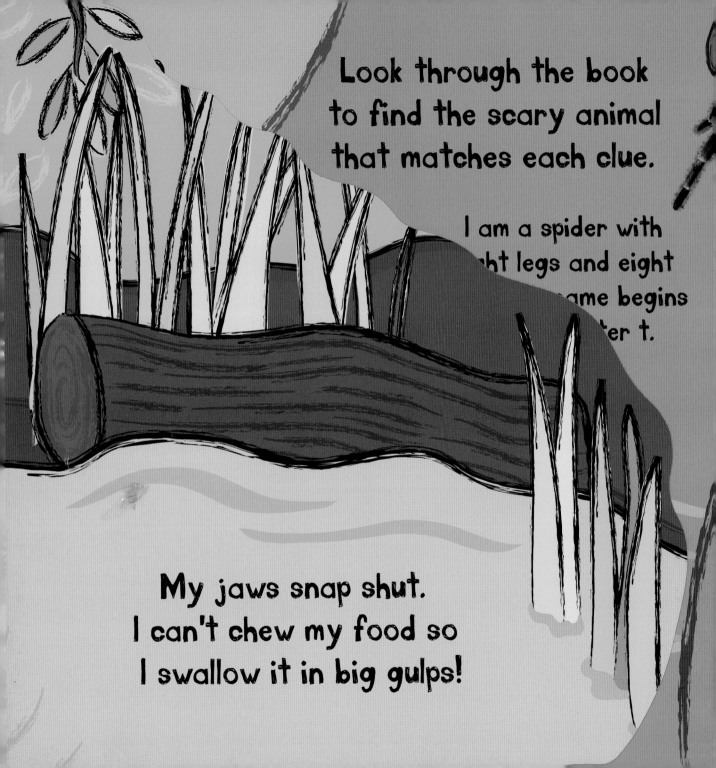

Make-a-monster

What do you think makes an animal scary?

Is it big teeth, sharp claws or big jaws?

Imagine a monster with lots of scary animal body parts.

Draw a picture of your monster and give it a really scary name.

Who's there?

Who is hiding in the forest?

Who is crawling on the ground?

Who is swimming in the water?

Next steps

The first time you read the book together, encourage your child to guess the identity of each animal before turning the flap. Talk together about how they guessed the animal's identity. Did they look at the picture, listen to the words, or use both sets of clues?

The second time you read the book together, encourage your child to read along with you, especially the repeated words and phrases, such as 'Who...', 'I do' and 'I am'.

Enjoy completing the activities together. You can do more research into the topic using the Internet and books from the library.

One reason animals look scary is to stay safe. Remind your child that very few animals harm people; most animals are scared of us and prefer to keep as far away as possible!

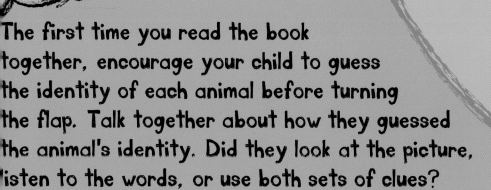